Ripe

Poetic Notes Written By: Melissa Michelle Jones

I dedicate this

To my family

To my friends

To my experiences

To love

Poetry has always been a personal outlet. I would be what you call a late bloomer when it came to knowing who I am and what I am capable of. It took me a long time to not only see the woman I've become let alone know who that woman even was. It took me some time to find my voice and even longer to figure out what to do with it once I finally heard it. That's my truth and my journey.

I take all my experiences as opportunities to grow, learn and overcome. We can't choose what necessarily happens to us but we can choose how we feel about it and what we do after the events in life have transpired.

I hope my words convey feelings of inspiration, memories and love. I hope you feel my love in every letter throughout this book. I have a few sections that require your participation. The goal is to include you in this very special project.

Thank you

From the very bottom of my heart

Xoxo,

Melissa

Ripe

Dear Daddy

They say your father is supposed to be your first love
Where were you as I stood outside in the cold
Waiting days, weeks, months for you to come home
When I needed you the most
To me you became a stranger
A man I wanted to know
Stranger
The title of my first published poem
I read it the other day and I wished you would've known
Your daughters heart you broke
How am I supposed to love a man
When I could barely find the first man I ever loved

The first man I looked up to and needed his hugs

The man who took me into the ocean

So deep the water was no longer blue

But I was safe cause dad I had you

All I ever wanted was you to choose

Me

Not what you needed

Not what you used

Just me

I was so angry with you, not realizing the battle you were facing was bigger than what I could have imagined. I just wish I was bigger than that battle you were facing. I wish it was my face you saw during that war. My face would be the key to your chains. My face should've broken those chains.

I wanted to be the white flag in the distance giving you hope. I wished you knew that there was peace in me and peace in us. I just wanted you to choose us.

It's hard to see the light in the dark and it was hard to see the crack that eventually broke your daughters heart.

You taught me pain but you also taught me strength and I am glad today I can say I still have you.

I am proud of who you've become.

Like it never happened

The battle of the mind and heart
The mind remembers everything
The heart remembers nothing

Pefectly Imperfect

How do I write about one of the most important people I know
How do you find the words to express
The woman that is you
My biggest supporter
With the heaviest shoulders
And the most open heart
I could list the things I would change
But you wouldn't be you
And I wouldn't be me
That would be ashame
I wish you would appreciate what you've achieved
And not the things you have yet to conquer
Let go of the past
Don't let life pass you
Live like there is no tomorrow
Be present
Enjoy lifes presents

Be open to love
Know that you did all you could
You are loved
Embrace your circle with nothing to prove
Because there's a wonderful woman inside of you
Who birthed 3 amazing souls
What an incredible thing to produce
I could never fault you for who you are
Or what you lack
You've been there through your depression
Always having my front and my back
I didn't search for perfection
I never expected that
I never expected more than what God has blessed me with
That is you
I just hope that when a child chooses my womb to be their birthplace
I do it with half your grace
Thank you

Same

Life has a way of getting to us
We make mistakes
Wrong decisions
Wake up hungover from having way too many
Next to strangers hoping you didn't give them any
Sometimes hurting others with our selfish ways
We may never get it together, failed yesterday and failed today

        We may wake up everyday feeling exactly the same

            Still doing the same unfortunate things

                It's up to you to make the change

Speed Racer

Sometimes we end up on a road leading to where
Not sure
Sometimes we end up there due to a detour

                          Sometimes it's the road we chose
Flat tires, scrapes, accidents
We work on the repairs, end up with paint jobs and oil changes
We keep going and continue driving on this open road if we are lucky
Some end up on roads where their miles have expired and left with no more road to see
Some end up with changed interiors, new engines and some trade out the old for the new
No one drives the same road
We all have different journeys on this earth
Faster or slower and others race through every checkpoint

                                  Some never get the point

Fork

We never know
If the road we chose
Will help us find our way home

<u>Strongest muscle ever</u>

There's something about always understanding

The certainty that you will always remain humane

No matter how much pain has been exchanged

The heart remains unaffected

The heart still beats the same

11:11

A sweet reminder of hope

Every night and every morning

Same time every day

Coincidence some would say

I believed it was something more

I believed and nothing more

Messages from heaven

Every time I glimpsed at the clock

There it was

11:11

12

At 12 I fell in love
But not in the conventional sense
Just within the innocence of my adolescence
During many encounters of words from my childhood friend
Mesmerized by his voice and vocabulary
Two children from different upbringings, different cities, different starts
His tempo was the rhythm of my heart
I was everything to him
He'll never know he was more to me
His rhymes were real to me
I vibed with his floetry
Even though at times it was above my maturity
Causing me to feel strange things within
Yet still this wasn't like the changes of becoming a woman
It was a transition to transcend
He challenged my mind and my thoughts
Left me a 12 year old open
It was the first time I could see
First time I truly felt
The emotion and creativity
That flowed through myself

<u>Misunderstood</u>

Many conversations can leave blank stares
No feedback or exchanging of words
Cause they lack the ability to share
Compassion is an emotion that can fall completely void
Whether the subject matter is heartache or about the most beautiful joy
Sometimes our deepest thoughts or feelings have to nestle in our souls
For no one to know
If you were to open up would they listen or fall upon the deaf and cold

Star - David - Nichelle

I'll never forget the first time I laid eyes on you
The innocence and purity of my view
All three times and each time felt new
Thankful for the births of you
Many miles I spend from you

Just know I'll always be here for you

Each day I see you grow
My love overflows
Sweet babies I love you more than you may know
All three of you I yearn to hold
Lullabies and stories told

                                        Just know this one thing is true
                                            I'll always be there for you

Masterpiece

You were created
An amazing creation
Due to this process
You now exist
Beautifully made
No man on earth can change this

<u>Beautiful</u>

The innocence of your love
You have no idea how beautiful you are
You have the world in your hands
And the stars in your heart
Nothing is impossible
No dream or no plan
Your smile and your tiny voice
Your pint size stature and poise
Your thoughts are refreshing
There is beauty in your hopes for the future
Please keep them and treasure
Even when the world becomes a little darker, windier and cold
Dress warmer and keep your eyes to the sky
Remember your light

<u>Picking up the pieces</u>

The broken pieces you see are like abstract is to artistry
You are not perfect but you were created beautifully
On purpose and yet you can't see what your worth is
Witnessing the situations you allow
Hurts more than what you see in yourself
It cuts deep knowing you gave birth to a child
Not just one but 3, yet you still don't see the bigger picture
It's not only you, every decision you make affects their future
What you see in the mirror they will forever compare to what life is supposed to be
Cause that's a reflection of Mommy
You're so smart and such a fighter
But somehow you diminish your flame
Don't let them contain your fire
Because of your pain and your trials
Please look at those kids and find your smile
Their innocence depends on your kiss
Your love for yourself and your love for them
Please see that you are resilient and please be the light to your children

I know it's not easy to do this alone. I could never imagine what you saw that last day you came home. Broken home. He decided he couldn't live without you, for you or for them. The saddest story I've ever known. His story ended but yours is still waiting to be told.

Missing Piece

I wish I could change the past

Bring back his laugh

Erase the pain

Inject the love within his veins

Within 3 he will forever remain

One decision and now the third sunday in June will never be the same

                                                  See something, do something

Something could change everything

Holla if you hear me

You ever feel disconnected
Like the world just doesn't get it
We speak the same language but they still don't comprehend it
I open my mouth but deaf ears fall upon it
I scream but just like an echo it's my own voice I am hearing
I am the only one listening

                                                    Can you hear me

Please listen

<u>Vulnerable</u>

I peel myself open
Myself I expose it
See me
Breathe me
Taste me
I give you this daily
Understand my intentions
The execution is effortless but still they shun
I can't hide truths or deliver lies
I can't fight for potential unless it's miles high
You'll continue to turn away and I'll continue to try

Mirror

I look within myself
I take responsibility for the loss
The pain
The let downs
The missed trains
It's so easy to blame everyone but you
Until you change your state of mind
That mind will be forever your truth

                                            It will mind you

Captive and amongst a place that lacks change
Growth is beautiful yet hard to explain
It frustrates the stubborn mental and falls deaf to their cries
They don't want to listen
Until you realize
That all it takes is for you to open your eyes
That amazing person inside you will arise

                                            Just open your eyes

Stranger

On the corner you sat and stared
I walked past you and a glimpse we shared
In the deep of the night you disappeared
Slithering down the dark street
Were you still there
No one could tell
But what you did know was that I was still in sight
In your eyes
This evenings prize
Unaware was this beautiful being
Approaching safe haven after a long days work
Home she was seeking
Lost in her thoughts of the day to day
Life in her hands
Lunch from today

Turn the key
Yes turn the knob
With no others around she felt a presence
She felt a throb
Between her legs this grip grew strong
All of her life spread all over the floor
The darkness had come right through her door
Her vulnerability enticing
You smelled it like fresh warm cake
You were ready with icing
Hoping your force would lay her on the ground
But in this woman there was strength and balance was found
She managed
She survived
A little bruising to the ego but no major damage
Forever knowing you took advantage

<u>Poker Face</u>

What do you do when no one knows your truth
They've never walked in your shoes
What do you do when everything doesn't add up to how it looks
All that is left is for them to assume
(ass out of you not me)
What you reveal to the world through a smile
Could hint that in your cards lies a queen

Figuratively Speaking

Figuring things out figuratively
It's easy to fill up with doubt and live a life uninspiring
To think we cannot touch our potential like it's something beyond our reach
Seeking peace
But how do you seek peace when you can't see the beauty beneath

You

Your turn - Here is where you write a poem or a few words where you've felt lost:

Sit with your thoughts and write about a time you've been misunderstood:

Share your story of someone you loved who hurt you - tell them how you feel:

Thank you for sharing. This work is incredibly amazing. I hope one day you'll share it with someone.

Just know, no matter what you have been faced with

You're still standing

You're still here to face another day

You're still here

Everything will be ok

Was and were

You were everything

You were supposed to be

It was supposed to be you and me

Your heart beat was my favorite melody

The inspiration to my greatest poetry

                                      I'll forever be grateful - thank you

~~You~~ Me

I wanted it to be you
I wanted to stay up all night laughing
Late evenings talking
Midnight dancing
I wanted you to light up from my smile
I wanted you to want me to stay over for more than a while
I wanted to make things all better by my presence
My warmth would be the cure for your lechery
I wanted you to protect me
Life without me would be something you couldn't imagine
I wanted you to be apart of my life
I wanted to be part of yours
I wanted to get flowers for no reason
Surprise visits in and out of seasons
I wanted you to be proud to have me
I wanted you to have me
I wanted you
When I should've wanted me

All I See Is You

The one thing I tell myself is to not lose my focus
But somehow my focus was you
So I adjusted my vision as I looked through the lens to focus my view
Others looking from outside in called me hopeless
Others said that I chose less
They told me no but it was you so I chose yes
I exposed my heart and I had nothing to hide nor confess
I was all the way down
Lost in you I was nowhere to be found
My last was yours first
The lack of your first was the worst
Till this day it still hurts
The concept of mine didn't exist
It was yours nobody else's
There it was
Still it is
All my love and the memories of what you will never miss

<u>Mine</u>

**Just because you are always on my mind
doesn't make you mine**

9 1 1

There's been an emergency
Her heart can't figure out what the eyes can see
There's a disconnection we need to put her in surgery ASAP
It all started with an accident between two strangers who collided on a map
Distance was nothing to these two persons who connected like magnets
She was pure of heart and he wanted to know what that felt like
He sucked from her honey and he played in her innocence
Making all his wrongs right
In this exchange of what some would say was foul play
Her play was foreplay and his intentions left her played
The star in this theatrical tragedy was him
No supporting actors
She became a mere fan better yet an aspiring actress
Auditioning for the role but never casted
He liked her position
Never allowing her to realize her position
Beneath him
Now she lays here in the hospital bed
With symptoms of ugly truths and beautiful lies
Cheated by love
Cheated by words
And cheated by time
Save her bring her back to life

Not mine

I won't have your first child
But I promise to love yours like my own
I'll never have the first cry
Nor the first birth or the first finger to hold

Fruitful

You called me gorgeous yet you lusted for my ripened fruit

Fruit that was only ripe for you

This is something you always knew

Mind reader

I wish I could read your mind
Are your train of thoughts sequential
Are they sporadic
Are your thoughts filled with fear or consistently erratic
To hurt another in a way that's perceived as selfish
Not ever allowing them to have a say in their own pain
How does that taste in your mouth
How cold is your heart
Is that organ you call a heart permanently detached
Do the signals in your brain never make it to your chest

You have a woman who only wants to love you
Somehow you are unable to reciprocate such an amazing embrace
Are you completely incapable
Does this frustrate you
Or are you ignorant to the situation at hand
I just wonder how you can look like one

But you can never call yourself a man

Perception I

Maybe it was all in my head
Creating words that were never said
So these words would be intentions never meant
Comfort in my ignorance
For years I felt content
Maybe these women were telling the truth
Or maybe it was always me
But never you

Tease me

Tell me your time is limited
I'm first in line yet your schedule is tentative
Tell me you can't see me too frequently
You don't want to get bored and you'd rather miss me
Touch me and leave your imprint within my walls
Deprive me of this feeling whenever my body calls
Share your world in pieces
Spare me of getting full off of you
Knowing what I can view is only surface deep
Baby tease me
Rarely please me
Give me a taste of what I'll never have
Let it drip on my lips of the one thing I want so bad
Tease me
Give me hope
Make me a believer
Give me a taste of something I will never have

Love can be a very fickle thing

But I'll go for it every single time

Hunger games

You don't want me
Why are you here
In my inbox
When you clearly don't really even care
Responding to messages at your leisure
No urgency or worry just enough to appease her
Keep her at bay
Keep her waiting
Keep her around
Keep her afloat 1 inch from the ground
You don't want me
Why are you here
A question I'll never know the answer to
The answer I once feared

<u>Perception II</u>

Her: he is my heart

Him: she is my tuesday

Don't take it personal

She said ignorance is bliss
As she viewed from the place she chose to stand
She was convenient and he was another womans' man

Her

Less of an obsession
More like a series of questions
In my mind and they linger in my heart
Does she love you like I do
Pray for you
Touch you like I could
Is she down for you like my love
Serenade you with her heart just because
She's pretty
Hope she provides more than that
It will take more than 34 on the top and 40 inches in the back
When you're with her do you think of me
As you lie with her do visions of me pop up in your mind like a tv screen
I can try to analyze over and over about your life without me
It took me a while to see
That she nor they or them will ever be
me

Threesome

I wanted to know why you
Everything about you
I knew
I fantasized about what you did in the times I wasn't there
Did he like your laugh
Did he play in your hair
I noticed similarities
I stared
I forever compared
Even when you moved on
Of course I knew
Of course I was aware
I still wonder did he hurt you
Did you love him too

Did he love you

Like I do

Heart*brake*

It's been four seasons
I've looked and searched for many reasons
To not look back
To not keep track
No matter what I kept tabs
The connection still lingers
My love never erased
I tried to bury it but in my dreams I continue to see your face
I want to run
I want to give up
Let go of it all
Along with the trust
It's been so long
To the world there is no us

My heart didn't get the memo
It still replays the very moment before I let go
To you I gave up
To me it was the day that I woke up
The years feel like days
Yesterday was mere hours begging to stay
I close my eyes to replay scenes from the past
While this organ in my chest rhythmic in movement
May cause me to shut down and crash
With each beat my mind questions
How much longer will this last

Since you tangerines have never tasted the same....

One Night

Let's share one night
Let's forget we said goodbye
Let's forget everything
Forget all the fights
Let's book this last minute flight
Let's forget the lies as we lie tonight
I just want to breathe you in
Touch every inch of my skin
Swim in the curves of my body
Admire the lines of my silhouette slowly
I'd give anything to feel you
To live in you
Even if it's just for the night

Distant memory

I am working on forgetting you
No more I miss you
No more hello
Working on goodbye
Tried to do it before
I tried a few times
You neglect my tries
I neglect your lies
For once in this love
I have to decide
I thought I had you once upon a time
I left you
I lost you
It's so sad that this rhymes

Love for myself must outweigh us
We have no love
We have no trust
All that is left are evaporated drops of lust
Waiting for you to end it
To make the inevitable not so tough
I got caught up
Hoping I was enough
I am working on forgetting you
The more I hold on
The more of me I continue to lose

Walking away was one of the hardest things I ever had to do.

I had to love myself before loving you.

To be honest how could my love be so true
When there were two people in this relationship
But when the sun shined through
The only shadow that appeared was a silhouette of you

<u>Going down</u>

You are not the only one to blame
In court I would be an accomplice named
I've chosen to take responsibility and side by side I'll share the shame
Yes, we failed this love but just know me and you we are not the same

It's kinda like this,
love yourself enough to love or love yourself enough not to

Drafts   (actual unsent email)

Just know if you said let's move forward forget the past and be together. I would have given you all of me and pieces of the old me. Pieces of me you would have learned to love again. I wanted you to choose me. I know now that I was never even a choice or consideration. It's hard to admit that to yourself but I had to. Wanting to be the only one. I'm always the only lonely one. Every time. I really wonder if we ever had anything at all. I know that what we had wasn't love. I refuse to believe it. So go be with whomever you're entertaining. There is always somebody. If you don't love them they surely love you. I don't care what they mean to you cause some how they always seem to mean more than me. I'm always the secret. Second best. That's ok. You don't want me. I don't know what I ever did to you for you to keep saying shit you don't mean. That shit hurts every time. Even when I'm guarded and I'm always waiting for it to hurt. I'm making a promise to be open to love at this point of my life. I have to move on. Kiss some frogs. Let someone choose me. Let someone see themselves in me. I'm so ready for something real. I'm ready to share my life. Be my complete self around someone. Please go your way and I'll go mine. I will not see any more messages from you. So don't even bother. No more weak moments for me. I'm going to work on not loving you, continue loving me. Letting this go. I forgive you and now I forgive myself.

Bye

Sent from my iphone - please excuse the brevity and typos*

You once knew

The woman you once knew is still there. She is just way more guarded now. She's finally a woman. She's still emotional. She cries when she's sad and when she's happy. She still is enamored by sunsets. She is still a hopeless romantic even if romance has been absent in her life. She still sees the best in people. Her glass is always half full even on days that don't go her way. She'll still make posters to cheer you on in hopes of making you smile. She wants to be free. She wants to love naturally. She's a lover. She was in love with a man whom she was unsure will ever be proud to call her his or love her the way she deserves.

Write it out and let those words live in the drafts folder

Some things are better left unsent

What a Beautiful Creation

Despite your negligence and your love
Or lack of
You made a woman out of me
My baby soft skin slightly hardened
My tears erupted less and less throughout the years
You made a woman out of me
You were the definition of what I wanted but you became my ultimate lesson
At the same time one of my many blessings
You made a woman out of me
I'll be a better lover
A lot more tougher
Resilient
More aware of self
Never entertaining those who treat me less
I hope that when you lay your eyes upon me
You see
The woman who is me

Moving on and moving forward….. It's never as easy as it sounds

There's still so much more work to be done but I'm waiting on love……

I wanted everything but you

and looked for everything like you

<u>Upon a star</u>

I know you're out there
Waiting for me
Counting the days
Everyday you prepare for me in your life
Everyday I am preparing to be your wife
I feel you on my skin
I feel you deep beneath where you live
We admire the same moon and the same stars
I dream of your days and where you are
How many miles baby
Is the distance between us near or far

<u>Please don't put it on repeat</u>

I am looking for a connection I can't explain
Awaiting someone who will never leave me and will be committed to stay
Expecting that one who's willing to wait
With no motive as to what he shall gain
The one who will not bring it back like repeat
Like dejavu and the pain in my heart that still speaks

Oh Love

In a world full of jealousy, greed, gluttony, evil and hatred
All that appeals to me is love
Can I only aspire to that
Forget the career
Forget all the money in this spinning sphere
Forget the success
Can I just work towards loving my soulmate forever
I want to challenge your mind
Inspire your time
Love you from morning to night
And do it all over again
Soothe your stress
Pray daily the lord keeps you blessed
And be the one you refer to as the best
I was put here to give hope to a soul
A soul that wasn't sure it still existed
Something so pure and untainted
In this place where 80% are jaded
Let my love cure your hurt
Kiss away your pain
Be your escape

Fire place

Let me be your comfort
Your happy place
Your warmth in the cold
I aspire to love purely
Wholeheartedly
All of me

Only in my dreams

There are no goosebumps
I haven't been waiting to exhale
Love has become a myth
A fairytale
I close my eyes and imagine what you would feel like
Hands on my thighs and my knees squeeze tight
Something so familiar yet I barely remember
Only time I arch my back is when my dreams become wet
They say it will come
But it's been months to come

Winter storm

Snowed in
Turn on some R&B
Slow dancing to making love endlessly
Marathon
Non-stop making love to me
Your skin on my skin
Sweat in between
You devour my body leaving nothing left of me

24 hours

All the hours in a day
Let's make love for all hours of the day
Instant gratification is not a stop on this journey
Take your time
Let your senses take control
Relax your mind and allow your body to release its soul
As these souls dance where many hearts dare not to go

Pressure

My heart beats through my chest
Pulsating through my body to my breast
Pressure builds lower than where I digest
I want to meet you in a quiet place
Give up the chase
Grip my derrière and grab my face
My river runs no safety vest
This tide comes in as the sun sets
I hope you can swim
Who cares who's around
Who cares about them
Swollen you are so push within
Fill my walls
I surrender
I am yours to call

Lust

I wanna feel sexy
In front of you
Away from you
I want you to just sit and stare at it
Take a moment and stare at this
Admire my hips
Licking your lips as they switch
Slowly reaching out to touch my skin
Noticing the work I've put in at the gym
Gods creation yet this is totally sin
Its getting harder to resist
This man knows I do this for me and not for him
Moving my waist to my favorite song
Moving away so the tension grows strong
Enticing you from the living room to the bed
Palms sweaty
Mouth wet
He's thinking please don't take too long
Come here and take that off
So I unclip to let everything drop
Bite my lip to signal him to come

A Magical Place

My vagina is magic
She's not pulling a bunny out of a hat trick
She powerful and she knows it
Exclusive yet elusive
Beautifully seductive
It would be a tragedy to lose this
Once you've experienced the fluidity of her oceanic bliss
With lips you yearn to french kiss
She'll have you questioning what kind of spell is this
My vagina is magic

Horse and Carriage

As a child we read stories and fairy tales that teach us
This gentleman named Prince Charming would save us
Save us from the evil fortress
What we now know as life
Everything would be happy from that day forward
You've gone through hell to be saved by a man
He, who would be your reward
Does this mean in this man you will find perfection
You would find your happy ending
What if he can't save you
But he could love you
What if he needs your strength to ward off evil
What if he's waiting for you to save him
What if he's just like you
Same issues
Same shoes
Neither made of glass
Both of you share similar stories
And a similar past
Let him love you all the way to never never land and back

<u>Love like this</u>

He's gonna love me like this
Just like this
As is
Same eyes
Same lips
He's gonna love me like this
My bare face and my morning kiss
He's gonna love me like this
Unshaved legs and my face makeup-less
He's gonna love me like this
My mixed emotions and pettiness
My baby voice and silliness
He's gonna love me like this
My outlandish questions only because I am inquisitive
My brand new projects and many lists
He's gonna love me like this
My tears of joy and my tears for the ones I love and miss
He's gonna love me like this
My love for beauty and life's gifts

He's gonna love me just like this

Thoughts

Who would have thought
You and I together in one thought
Sweet on you as an adolescent
Yet your rejection left its remnants on my chest
Your denial and your decision to resist
I felt a little twinge in my heart
Moved on
Grew up
New start
Many years have passed
That was the past
It has passed
We created pages in our book of life
Experienced some wrongs and some rights
Tonight I lay here staring in your eyes
Who would have thought you and I
 In one thought as we lie

Not ready

I say it aloud
I am ready
Ready for love
Ready to be loved
I say it aloud
I am ready
Here you are a man
Ready to love
For me, you are ready
A past phone call
A phone call from the past
A slight imperfection
A speed going a little too fast
Causing a change of emotion in my body
I flatline and crash
Like a crab I curl up in my shell
I say it aloud
I am ready
The lies I continue to tell

You're amazing he says

not knowing the demons you fight in your head

When you left

Your essence remained on my skin

Imprints of you in the bed I lay in

Love at First Kiss

That moment
Your kiss was more than I expected
It felt like home
It soothed my soul
Awakened my heart
Without words our spirits said hello
The chills were physical evidence of the sparks that electrified through my body
The warmth of the flame
The warmth in my heart
Igniting the fire that grew from your touch
This kiss was perfection
Our lips in sync
Emotions ran high and raced against my heartbeat
Practically beating out of my chest cavity
Please be something I wont regret
I wanted you
I wanted your conquest

Sweet November

He's getting everything you once knew
Everything you remember
Sweet November
When you thought that girl was gone
The one you once pursued
He found her
Under the dust
She was found renewed

<u>After the war</u>

The fear that you'll refuse my touch
That my touch will turn you off
I forgive my past
But that's something you can't get past
Would have never thought I'd be a casualty of love
Giving my heart led to pain and scars
Loss of believing in the strength of men
Something I now fear is someone who will look past my gentle truths
And embody love and understanding
Seems too good to be true

<u>Where art thou?</u>

Oh love where art thou
I feel you in the distance
I hear your gentle whispers
I filter out the many who try cause their efforts fell short of this
This who is me
Me awaiting you
My heart is yearning
Tears have surfaced as the sun disappears but dry as dawn is born again
Another morning hoping to see your face
Another morning awaiting your embrace

C'mon Baby

Let's keep making love until we make a baby
C'mon baby
Maybe just maybe
You'll be my baby
C'mon baby call me your lady
Maybe just maybe
Don't keep me waiting
C'mon on baby you're driving me crazy
Maybe just maybe
Tell me you'll save me
Make me your baby

<u>Well traveled Man</u>

Home became a place to my right

He remained side to side

By my side

But when he traveled

He traveled deep

So deep inside

My panties weeped and cried

Behind closed doors

This was so far left
From one night this started
A few months in I tried to run
You stayed patient
You've been waiting
For my kiss
For every chance
Every chance not to miss
We danced in the shadows
Under sheets
Wherever night smirked
And when the morning weeps
I began to see you
The comfort in your eyes
The warmth in your touch
The genuineness that seeped out your pores
The love bursting and waiting to erupt
You saw me
The one they said you would never have
The one who now makes you laugh
The one who is not only a friend but a confidant
The one you admire and your forget me knot
The light is pouring in through the cracks
There's less fight to keep this under wraps

                                                          My little secret…

<u>Just not that into you</u>

                                                Who am I to steal your time
                                  Better yet waste it based on a lie
                                                      I' am not interested
                                                        I won't even try
                            But I entertain you just to keep my heart alive

<u>Its me not you</u>

I get impatient
For what he did I want you to pay for it
Everything we used to have
I want you to now replace it
Late replies and everything he denied
Ignites past lies and thoughts of past lovers
I'm sorry for having you try on shoes that weren't made for you
I find everything wrong when it's all right
All you want is to be my baby
The man by my side
Factors in my life that no one before has tried

Never thought I have to be the one to lose you
But it was you I couldn't choose
I had to face my truth
I stare at you but the look in your eyes reads confused
What we had I did everything in my power not to refuse
Closed my eyes and squeezed so tight but love I couldn't produce
The one thing we never want to hear is
It's me not you

Wrong turn

The tables have turned
You used to be abused
Now you're doing the abusing
Leading, teasing and using
Picking up hearts just to throw away
Each one never worth a try
They could never make you stay
Wrong fit
Wrong size
Moving swiftly as soon as the sun disappears and the day is full of night
Knowing that no matter how much he tried
He'd never be right

Where did it all go wrong?

<u>Choosy lover</u>

Option A:
You give me a feeling I can't describe
Your kisses do things to me that electrifies
Sending signals all over my body ending between my thighs
Every time
The way you say my name drives me completely insane
You're so sure of yourself and it's so refreshing
No matter where this goes just know you never cease to amaze me

Option B:
One kiss landed us here
One kiss and you changed my perspective
You're amazing and no one can compare
Your passion and the kindness in your stare
I could look in your eyes and become forever lost
but safe knowing that you're here and I am there
With you
The history within you I am obsessed with
Every conversation is an educational lesson
Just know that you are a blessing

I just know that one day I'll have to lose cause one day I'll have to choose

Bad Timing

We met where it's sunny
I was taken and you were ready
I was unhappy but you weren't steady
It felt right but halfway you never met me
Pursuit of my heart was a destination
A location on the map you couldn't see
I was the lock but you weren't my key
You weren't part of my puzzle
You weren't the missing piece
As good as it felt when we connected
Connected immediately
You weren't ever part of the plan
It wasn't bad timing
I am the woman and you weren't my man
We weren't meant to be
But my congratulations to you and your wife
Now your love is complete

Ego

All I want is the tables to turn
I want you to want me
Just so I can let it burn

Perfection is over rated

Give me challenges

High fives for resolutions

Rings and Shiny Things

I look and I wonder how lucky they must be
That the lover chose her and he got on one knee
I wonder when he knew and how he planned to make her his forever
Her one and only man
Were they best friends
Was it a beautiful romance
Did they laugh all night long and do a kitchen floor slow dance
Will I ever get the chance to look down at my hands
And smile while memories replayed in my head
Will that ever be in my plans
Will I ever find love in one man
As I glance
Wondering if she thought it was in her plans as she smiles at the diamond on her hand

Love my scars

They are the braille to my story

They aren't something the eyes can see nor the eyes can read

They tell a story that only the heart can feel

Remember your scars tell your story but do not define who you are

                          And that is when you will truly heal

The fear of being in no man's land where no one understands.

Never lose your hope

Continue to move forward

Continue to love

Continue to be great

When it's your time

When it's your moment

Just know that when it happens it will be on time and never late

I wish greatness to the very person reading these words

You are incredible

Please don't think anything less

Let's stop obsessing over someone else's blessings and start using our desires as motivation. Let another person's success motivate you. Their blessings are for them and yours are for you.

You and only you. Own it and embrace it. We tend to look at others and admire from the outside. What makes your challenges any different from theres?

Yes, they may have different struggles but they face challenges just like you and I. Just know you are just as beautiful and just as amazing.

What's behind door #1?

You ever wonder what's next
What is ahead on this journey we are on
You ever want to pull the curtain back
Cause the anticipation can be too difficult to endure
What is behind curtain #1
What's behind that door
You may ask
Is this something I am prepared for
Is this next chapter euphoric or mediocre
Have I done everything in my power to be ready
Am I ready for these unborn series of moments
Whatever is behind what I cannot see
I pray it's the most beautiful unveiling

Pack Light

Why do we look for an issue before there is actually an issue
When all I want is to let go and be with you
All I want is something real
Something true
But these days that's the issue
It also doesn't help when your past text you
I miss you
Everything in you wants to move on to what's new
But I steadily fixate on what came before instead of what's standing in front of me
Which is you
That baggage will hold you down if you let it
Make you regret it if you can't forget it
It will weigh you down when you're trying to fly
So I recommend that you pack light…

Some call it success

Will I make it
I put myself in a room
Close enough to taste it
My dreams am I brave enough to chase them
Still often I wonder
Will I make it
Making it is up to you to define
I fell off the road many times
Came across a few dead ends in my life
Again I ask will I make it knowing how hard I've tried
The question really isn't will I make it
The answer is not where you think it lies
The truth is in the belief that you've already made it

Now what will you do once you've made it

You're number one

I've loved you from the very beginning
In my eyes you could never lose
From day one I had visions of you winning
From your first failure to your first triumph
Each time I am silently cheering you on
Such a beautiful being
A woman who was perceived as weak but what you have endured reads a woman so strong
Your smile is contagious
It's amazing how you can even find the energy to frown
It was hard watching you experience the defeat that eventually put you down
It hurt even more when you let others manipulate you into removing your crown
Treating you as if you didn't matter
Treating you as if you couldn't inspire peace just from your laughter
I couldn't wait until you could see
I couldn't wait until the day you finally woke up and looked in the mirror to see what I've always seen

Me

Staring back
There I stand
Your reflection
Your biggest fan

Sweet memories. Sweet indeed. All the laughs, the tears, and the times when you didn't know such a thing as fear. The cringe worthy moments, everything you'll forever remember and the times you wish you could forget. Late night skinny dipping and winter storms with coffee cups full of rum and juice. Angels left in the commons. Sweet memories.

Pot Luck

A love without conditions
So often we fight and become conditioned
The closest of enemies we continue to grow
We really should be loving one another
And letting things go
For none of us had the choice
We were chosen
Bloodlines entangled
Connected as so
Pleading for change within the hearts and eyes
The seats still arranged back to back
Not side to side
There is power in us
If we just could see it
Nurture the development and continue to feed it
To realize all the beauty we create
The generations
The DNA
The ships haven't sailed
We still have a chance
We can still relate
Lets start with a dinner, pull up a chair and grab a plate

The Journey

We try to imagine what's coming
Wondering what's to come for me
Facing windfall of defeats and clear skies
Filled with moments of success
Being prepared for more
Trying to avoid less
The challenge is to remain focused
Seek progress
If we choose the right road
What will be of the road we chose
If the journey ahead can't be seen and is still waiting to unfold

Never apologize for being you. You are wonderfully made and created with a purpose.

Your plan is defined and devine.

Never forget how beautiful you are.

How amazing it is to be in your presence.

www.ingramcontent.com/pod-product-compliance
Lightning Source LLC
Chambersburg PA
CBHW070619050426
42450CB00011B/3082